Jesse Tree Kit

**An Advent Project
for Family, Classroom,
or Parish**

By Lynn M. Simms
and Betsy Walter

Pauline
BOOKS & MEDIA

Boston

ISBN 0-8198-3986-8

Cover photo by Mary Emmanuel Alves, FSP

Third edition

Published by Pauline Books & Media, 50 Saint Paul's Avenue, Boston, MA 02130-3491. www.pauline.org

Printed in Canada.

Pauline Books & Media is the publishing house of the Daughters of St. Paul, an international congregation of women religious serving the Church with the communications media.

1 2 3 4 5 6 7 8 9   14 13 12 11 10 09 08 07 06

Contents

The Story of the Jesse Tree

The symbol of the Jesse Tree comes from Isaiah 11: "The royal line of David is like a tree that has been cut down; but just as new branches sprout from a stump, so a new king will arise from among David's descendants." The tree is named after Jesse, the father of the great King David of the Old Testament.

In Church art a design developed which illustrated the relationship of Jesus with Jesse and other biblical personages. This design showed a branched tree growing from a reclining figure of Jesse. The various branches had pictures of other Old and New Testament figures who were ancestors of Jesus. Some trees also incorporated early Old Testament figures like Abraham and Moses, who lived long before Jesse's time. At the top of the tree were images of Mary and Jesus. This design was used mostly in stained glass windows in some of the great medieval cathedrals of Europe.

Another development in religious art during the Middle Ages was that of Mystery Plays—drama that depicted various Bible stories or lives of saints and martyrs. These plays were performed in churches as part of the liturgical celebrations. One such play was based on the biblical account of the fall of Adam and Eve. The "Tree of Life" used during the play was decorated with apples. (Quite possibly this is also the forerunner of our own Christmas tree.)

This kit draws from elements of both the Jesse Tree window and the Tree of Life. Each ornament symbolizes a person or event in *salvation history*—the pattern of events in human history that accomplishes the saving action of God. By reflecting on salvation history, we see how God prepared the world for the coming of his Son.

Jesse Trees are meant to symbolize the spiritual heritage of Jesus, rather than his strictly genealogolical origins. It is important to keep in mind that the Christian application of the Old Testament stories and symbols used does not minimize their own intrinsic value as Revelation.

Your Own Jesse Tree

The Jesse Tree is a very versatile project. It may be used by parents to highlight the true meaning of Christmas for their children. Teachers may wish to incorporate the Jesse Tree into their religious instruction classes during the Advent Season. The Jesse Tree tradition can also be adapted for a parish-wide celebration. Each week's symbols and Scripture readings can be copied and distributed to all the children of the parish to be worked on at home. The children can participate in the Advent services by bringing their completed ornaments to church, where they can be used to decorate a large Jesse Tree set up in the sanctuary or other appropriate area.

It will take planning and work from each family member or student to make your own Jesse Tree. The needed materials are usually found around most homes and classrooms.

First of all, you will need a Bible. If very young children will be involved, a Bible picture storybook will help them understand the biblical stories used.

This kit offers you two options. *Option 1* involves preparing an actual tree and decorating pre-drawn ornaments—one for each day of Advent. Please see page 5 for *Option 1* instructions.

Option 2 provides you with a Jesse Tree poster to which the ornaments may be attached. It is especially suitable for use in settings with limited space. Please turn to page 6 for *Option 2* instructions.

Once your ornaments are made you may wish to use the prayer service on page 13 for the hanging ceremony.

Be creative, have fun and enjoy your Jesse Tree. It's a beautiful way to share in the retelling of the greatest story of all!

Jesse Tree with Pre-Drawn Ornaments

The tree itself can be one of several types. A small evergreen tree—live or artificial—works fine, as does a tree branch (suggestive of a family tree) that is anchored in a bucket or a large can of sand or gravel. The tree branch looks particularly attractive if painted white and sprinkled with silver glitter while the paint is still wet.

At the back of this book, you will find twenty-eight symbol/ornaments, one for every day of Advent. (Note: The length of the Advent Season varies from year to year. The longest Advent can be is twenty-eight days, the shortest, twenty-one days. The choice of which ornaments to exclude when Advent is less than twenty-eight days is left up to parents and teachers.) Each ornament represents a person or event in biblical history, from creation to the birth of Jesus. Seven ornament designs are arranged on each of four pages for easy photocopying. This format meets the needs of teachers who gather with their students only once a week. Each group of seven symbols can be covered during one of the four classes in Advent. Beginning on page 7 you will find a biblical passage and brief explanation to accompany every ornament.

To decorate the ornaments you will need crayons, markers, paints, or colored pencils. For use on a

FOR OPTION 1

tree, both sides of the ornaments will need to be colored in. Use a paper punch to make a hole at the top of each ornament. Use ribbon or yarn (preferably purple) to hang the ornaments on your tree.

Jesse Tree Poster
with Pre-Drawn Ornaments

When you don't have room for an actual tree, the ornaments can be cut out, colored and taped or glued to the branches of the fold-out tree poster included in this kit. In this case, only the front sides of the ornaments need to be colored in. The numbered circles on the poster show the order in which to "hang" the ornaments—from the lowest branch to the Baby Jesus on top. If the activity is used at home, children can color in the ornaments while their parents read them the stories of how our ancestors waited for the Savior. As Christmas approaches, the tree poster will become progressively covered with the biblical symbols.

One final word on the symbols themselves: use them any way you wish. They may be colored with crayons, felt-tip markers, colored pencils or embellished in any way you choose. You can glue them to cardboard to make them more durable or cover them with clear contact paper and preserve them from year to year. For those who are even more ambitious, the designs can also be used as a pattern to transfer the symbols to wood or felt.

FOR OPTION 2

The First Week of Advent

Scripture Verses

The symbols for our Jesse Tree start with the first stories found in the Bible—God's creation of the world and of Adam and Eve. Next is the wonderful story of Noah and his ark full of animals.

The saga of God's chosen people begins with the promises he made to Abraham, Isaac, and Jacob. God's concern for his people is expressed again through the story of Joseph and his coat of many colors.

1. *Creation*—Read Genesis 1:26–31

In the beginning...God created the universe, the sun, moon, and stars. He created our beautiful world and filled it with all kinds of plants and animals. Last of all he created the first man and woman. This was the beginning of the human family, the original source of everyone's family tree.

2. *Adam and Eve*—Read Genesis 3:1–7

The first man and woman God created were Adam and Eve and he set them in the Garden of Eden. They were God's greatest creations because he gave them a mind to know the difference between good and evil, a will to make choices with, and a soul that would live forever. But they disobeyed God by eating of the fruit of the tree of the knowledge of good and evil, and God banished them from paradise.

3. *Noah*—Read Genesis 6:11–22; 9:8–13

Many generations after Adam, when all the people had turned away from God, there lived a man named Noah. Because Noah was good and obeyed God, God saw to it that he and his family and all the animals he had gathered onto his ark would survive the great flood God was sending to remove all evildoers from the earth and give the world a new beginning.

4. *Abraham and Sarah*—Read Genesis 12:1–7 and Hebrews 11:8

The history of God's chosen people begins with Abraham and Sarah. In faith Abraham obeyed God's command to leave his home country. He left not knowing where he would go. But he believed that God would fulfill his promise to give him a new land and descendants as numerous as the stars.

5. *Isaac and Rebecca*—Read Genesis 22:1–7

When Abraham was an old man, his faith was finally rewarded with the birth of a son, Isaac. It seemed God's promise of making him the father of a great nation was to be fulfilled. But then one day God told Abraham to take Isaac and offer him as a sacrifice. Abraham loved his son but he trusted God. At the last moment God stopped him and provided a ram to be killed in Isaac's place.

FOR OPTION 2

6. *Jacob and Rachel*—Read Genesis 28:10–22

One of Isaac's sons was Jacob. One day Jacob had a dream. He saw a ladder stretching from earth to heaven with angels going up and down it. In the dream God told Jacob he would become the father of a great people with a land of their own. From Jacob's twelve sons came the people of Israel, the people from which Jesus came.

7. *Joseph*—Read Genesis 37:1–4

Jacob's favorite son was Joseph, and one day he gave him a coat of many colors. Joseph's eleven brothers were jealous, and so they kidnapped him and sold him into slavery in Egypt. There, with God looking after him, Joseph rose to a position of power. Later, during a famine in that part of the world, Jacob, along with Joseph's repentant brothers and their families, came to live in Egypt where Joseph had stored enough food for them all.

The Second Week of Advent

Our first symbol for the second week of Advent represents Moses, the leader of the Jewish people during their great exodus from slavery in Egypt. He was helped in this endeavor by his brother Aaron. The story of their search for the Promised Land continued with Joshua and the battle of Jericho. Later, God again intervened by sending his people Samson, a leader of incredible strength.

The symbols for our tree continue with the beautiful story of Ruth and her grandson Jesse, after whom this tree is named. The final symbol is that of the greatest Jewish king, David, in whose line Jesus was to be born.

8. *Moses*—Read Exodus 20:1–17

It was during the time when the people of Israel had become slaves in Egypt that God saved the life of a little Hebrew baby who was placed in a basket among the reeds of a river. The baby was Moses, and when he was grown, God chose him to lead the Hebrew people out of Egypt and slavery. In the desert on the way to the Promised Land, Moses climbed Mount Sinai. There God gave him the Ten Commandments, the laws God wants us all to obey.

9. *Aaron*—Read Exodus 5:22, 11:5

God told Moses to let his brother Aaron speak for him in trying to persuade the Pharaoh to let the Hebrew people leave Egypt. To show how powerful his God was, Aaron threw down his rod before the Pharaoh and it became a serpent, swallowing up the serpents that had been produced by the Pharaoh's magicians and sorcerers.

10. *Joshua*—Read Joshua 6:20

Moses died before he got to the Promised Land, and Joshua was appointed the new

FOR OPTION 2

8

leader of the Hebrew people. Joshua planned to capture the city of Jericho. He ordered the Israelites to march around the city seven times. Then, when the priests blew their trumpets and the people shouted, the walls of the mighty city fell.

11. *Samson*—Read Judges 16:21–30

Years later, the Israelites became enslaved by the Philistines, and God sent them a new leader with incredible strength, Samson. After winning many victories for his people, Samson was tricked and captured. Taken to the pagan temple of the Philistines, Samson stood between two pillars and knocked them down, causing the destruction of the temple and all the Philistines who were inside it.

12. *Ruth*—Read Ruth 1:15–18

The symbol of gathered wheat stands for Ruth who collected grain from the fields of an Israelite farmer in Bethlehem. She was a foreigner who had married a Hebrew, and after his death she took care of his mother Naomi and remained faithful to his God. Later she married the farmer in whose fields she worked, and God rewarded her goodness by sending her a son, Obed. Obed became the father of Jesse and the grandfather of the great Jewish king David.

13. *Jesse*—Read Isaiah 11:1–2

Many years after Jesse lived, the prophet Isaiah would foretell the coming of the Messiah and would trace Jesus' ancestry back to Jesse. "There shall come forth a shoot from the stump of Jesse, and a branch shall grow out of his roots." And so it was in the family line of Jesse that Jesus Christ was born in fulfillment of the prophecies.

14. *David*—Read Samuel 5:1–5

The star of David has come to represent the nation of Israel. As a shepherd boy, David's faith in God enabled him to slay the giant Goliath. Later he became a king and ruled Jerusalem for thirty-three years. He was a great king because he trusted God and tried to obey him. David made some mistakes, but he continued to turn to God for fogiveness and guidance, and Israel became a strong nation under his leadership.

The Third Week of Advent

The Jesse Tree symbols for the third week of Advent start with the wise King Solomon. He is followed by two great prophets, Elijah, who was carried up to heaven in a chariot of fire, and Isaiah, who foretold the birth of Jesus.

God again reveals his loving concern for us in the stories of Daniel, who was spared death in the lions' den, and Jonah, who survived three days in the belly of a whale.

As we approach the time of Jesus, we learn the story of Zechariah and Elizabeth, the parents of John the Baptist. John was the prophet who preached the coming of the Messiah and baptized Jesus himself.

15. *Solomon*—Read 1 Kings 3:3–14

Solomon followed his father, David, as king of Israel. God had offered Solomon anything he wished for and was pleased when instead of riches or glory Solomon asked for wisdom to rule his kingdom. Solomon is also remembered for the beautiful temple he built for God in Jerusalem. The temple served the people of Israel as the central place of worship for over 350 years.

16. *Elijah*—Read 2 Kings 2:11–18

The prophet Elijah lived 900 years before Jesus at a time when Israel was ruled by weak kings, and the people worshipped false gods. God gave Elijah much spiritual power to convince the Israelites to return to their true God. When his job on earth was done, God sent a chariot of fire that swept Elijah up to heaven in a whirlwind.

17. *Isaiah*—Read Isaiah 2:4; 7:14; 9:6–7

Isaiah, another great prophet of the Old Testament, lived near the city of Jerusalem about 700 years before Christ. He gave hope to the Israelites that peace would come to their nation, "and they shall beat their swords into plowshares." He also foretold the birth of a child who would be called "Emmanuel," which means "God is with us." This child was Jesus.

18. *Daniel*—Read Daniel 6:10–23

Daniel was among the people of God who were captured by King Nebuchadnezzar and taken to Babylon. There Daniel became a friend and advisor to the king. One day, the king was tricked by jealous nobles into signing a law that condemned Daniel to death. For praying to his God, Daniel was thrown into the lions' den. But Daniel was not harmed. God answered his prayers and sent an angel to shut the lions' mouths.

19. *Jonah*—Read Jonah 1–4

Jonah was told by God to go to the city of Nineveh to warn the people to turn away from their wicked ways. Instead of obeying God, Jonah tried to run away. He boarded a ship, but God sent a storm and Jonah was tossed overboard and swallowed by a whale. Jonah lived within the whale for three days, praying to God to forgive him. Finally, the whale spit him out on dry land. This time, Jonah obeyed and preached God's message so well that all the people of Nineveh repented and were saved.

20. *Zechariah and Elizabeth*—Read Luke 1:5–23

Elderly Zechariah and his wife Elizabeth (who was Mary's cousin) prayed for many years for God to give them a child. One day an angel appeared to Zechariah and told him Elizabeth would bear him a son who was to be named John. John would be the prophet promised by God to help prepare the people for the coming of the Savior. Because Zechariah could not believe what the angel told him, he was made mute and could not speak until after his son was born.

FOR OPTION 2

21. *John the Baptist*—Read Matthew 3:1–11

Six months before Jesus was born, Elizabeth gave birth to a son and she and Zechariah named him John, just as the angel had instructed. When John grew up he preached that the people should repent of their sins and be baptized. He baptized hundreds of people, including his cousin, Jesus. This is how he became known as John the Baptist. John's symbol is the shell.

The Fourth Week of Advent

The symbols for the fourth week of Advent all deal with the people involved with the miraculous birth of Jesus. We start with the parents of Mary, Anne and Joachim, who brought Mary up in the readiness to always do God's will. This prepared her to accept God's invitation to become the mother of his Son. Joseph lovingly fulfilled his role as the husband of Mary and the protective foster father of Jesus.

The little town of Bethlehem, with its mysterious star, was the setting for Jesus' birth. The shepherds in the fields were the first to hear the news proclaimed by the angels who filled the sky. And so it was that Jesus came to be born, closing the final chapter of the saga that had begun so long ago. And yet his birth is also the beginning of a new and even more wonderous story for all people.

22. *Anne and Joachim*

According to tradition, Anne and Joachim were the parents of Mary, the mother of Jesus. The book is the symbol of the way St. Anne taught Mary. It was from her that Mary heard the story of the chosen people and of the Messiah who was to save the whole world. Little did Mary realize that one day God would choose her to be the mother of his Son.

23. *Mary*—Read Luke 1:26–38

God sent the angel Gabriel to Mary in Nazareth. Gabriel told her the Lord was with her and that she was chosen among all women to bear God's Son, the king of all people, whom she should name Jesus. Mary answered, "I am the Lord's servant. May it happen to me as you have said." The symbol of a loving heart represents Mary, our mother in heaven.

24. *Joseph of Nazareth*—Read Matthew 1:18–25

Joseph, a descendant of King David, worked as a carpenter. While he was engaged to Mary, an angel appeared to him and told him that Mary had conceived a son by the power of the Holy Spirit and that this son would be the Messiah. Joseph agreed to take Mary as his wife, as the angel instructed, and he loved and protected Jesus, the Son of God, as his foster son.

25. *Star of Bethlehem*—Read Matthew 2:1–6

Many years before, the prophet Micah had predicted that from the town of Bethlehem a ruler would come who would save Israel. And so it happened that a census was ordered and Mary and Joseph had to travel to Bethlehem to be taxed.

They stayed in a stable because there was no room for them in the inn. And while they were there Mary gave birth to Jesus. That night a special bright star shone in the sky over the place where Jesus was.

FOR OPTION 2

26. *Shepherds*—Read Luke 2:8–20

On the night Jesus was born, there were some shepherds in the fields keeping watch over their flocks. An angel appeared to them and told them their Savior had been born. They hurried off and found Mary and Joseph and saw Baby Jesus lying in a manger. The shepherds were the first to welcome Jesus, and they went away singing praises to God for all they had heard and seen.

27. *Angel*—Read Luke 2:8–14

The angel of the Lord who appeared to the shepherds announced: "I bring you good news of great joy for all the people, for unto you is born in the city of David, a Savior, who is Christ the Lord." Suddenly the sky was filled with a great choir of angels, singing their praise to God: "Glory to God in the highest, and on earth peace and good will to all people."

28. *Jesus*—Read Luke 2:1-20

And so it was that Jesus, God's Son, came to be born in Bethlehem. He was the Messiah whose coming had been predicted by the prophets and long awaited by the people of Israel. As the star shone down from on high, Jesus lay in his manger bed, the greatest sign of God's infinite love for his people.

Jesse Tree Prayer Service

When the family or class has gathered around the tree or poster for the service, the person who decorated the symbol for the day reads the accompanying Scripture verse and explanation. Parents or an older child can read for a younger child. Use either a Bible or Bible storybook for the reading. Pass around the ornament for all to see. Then the person who decorated the day's ornament may hang it on the tree or poster.

Another family or class member then reads the prayer for the current week of Advent.*

After the Advent prayer all can pray silently or share prayer aloud for a few minutes.

Close the service with a familiar Advent hymn.

Advent Prayers

First Week of Advent

O Lord, stir up your power and come! Rescue us from sin and all evil by your holy protection. Help us to prepare our hearts for your Son's new coming in grace this Christmas. We ask this through Christ our Lord, who lives and reigns with you and the Holy Spirit, one God, forever and ever. Amen.

Second Week of Advent

Lord, give us pure hearts and minds as we await the coming of your Son. Increase our hope. We praise and thank you for all the good things you have done and continue to do for us. May we serve you and one another in the love Jesus came to earth to bring. We ask this through Christ our Lord. Amen.

Third Week of Advent

Lord, please hear our prayers. May we always rejoice in your redeeming love. Open our eyes to the goodness around us and grant us the light of your grace that we may never be overcome by the darkness of sin. We ask this of you through Jesus our Lord. Amen.

Fourth Week of Advent

Heavenly Father, help us to celebrate Jesus' coming in joy and peace. May we welcome him into our lives in a new way this Christmas, allowing him to love and act in and through us. Help us to be like Mary, always ready and eager to do your will. Increase our faith and love. We ask all this through Christ our Lord, who lives and reigns with you and the Holy Spirit, one God, forever and ever. Amen.

(* From December 17–23 the "O" Antiphon takes the place of the Advent prayer or can be used in addition to the weekly prayer if desired.)

The "O" Antiphons

December 17

   O Wisdom, you come out of the mouth of the Most High. You reach from one end of the earth to the other, and keep all things in order by your power and your kindness; come and teach us prudence.

December 18

   O Lord and Leader of Israel, you appeared to Moses in the burning bush and gave him the Law on Mount Sinai: come with outstretched arms and redeem us.

December 19

   O Flower of Jesse, you are a sign for all the people of God's love for us. Kings keep silence before you and gentiles pray to you: come quickly to deliver us.

December 20

   O Key of David and Scepter of the house of Israel, you open and no one can close, you close and no one can open: come and rescue us who are the prisoners of darkness and death.

December 21

   O Radiant Dawn, brightness of light eternal and Sun of Justice: come and enlighten us who sit in the darkness of sin and the shadow of death.

December 22

   O King of the Gentiles, you are the one who is desired by all people. You are the capstone that makes both Israel and the gentiles one: come and deliver us, the race you formed from the dust of the earth.

December 23

   O Emmanuel, our King and Lawgiver, you are the expected one of all nations and their Savior: come to save us, O Lord our God.

December 24

Prayer for Christmas Eve

   O God, you fill us with happiness each year as we wait for our celebration of Christmas. May we also joyfully look forward to the coming of Jesus as our final Judge. We ask this of you through Jesus our Lord. Amen.

An Advent Hymn

O Come, O Come, Emmanuel

O come, O come Emmanuel,
Come, ransom captive Israel,
Which mourns in lonely exile here
Till Christ, the Son of God, appear.

> *Refrain:*
>
>> Rejoice! Rejoice! Emmanuel
>> Shall come to you, O Israel!

O come, O Wisdom from on high,
Who order all things mightily;
The path of knowledge to us show,
And teach us in her ways to go. *Refrain.*

O come, O Key of David, come,
Come open wide our heav'nly home;
Make safe the way that leads to you,
And close the path to sorrow, too. *Refrain.*

Pauline
BOOKS & MEDIA

The Daughters of St. Paul operate book and media centers at the following addresses. Visit, call, or write the one nearest you today, or find us on the World Wide Web, www.pauline.org

CALIFORNIA

3908 Sepulveda Blvd., Culver City, CA 90230	310-397-8676
5945 Balboa Ave., San Diego, CA 92111	619-565-9181
2640 Broadway Street, Redwood City, CA 94063	650-369-4230

FLORIDA

145 S.W. 107th Ave., Miami, FL 33174	305-559-6715

HAWAII

1143 Bishop Street, Honolulu, HI 96813	808-521-2731
Neighbor Islands call:	800-259-8463

ILLINOIS

172 North Michigan Ave., Chicago, IL 60601	312-346-4228

LOUISIANA

4403 Veterans Memorial Blvd., Metairie, LA 70006	504-887-7631

MASSACHUSETTS

Rte. 1, 885 Providence Hwy., Dedham, MA 02026	781-326-5385

MISSOURI

9804 Watson Rd., St. Louis, MO 63126	314-965-3512

NEW JERSEY

561 U.S. Route 1, Wick Plaza, Edison, NJ 08817	732-572-1200

NEW YORK

150 East 52nd Street, New York, NY 10022	212-754-1110

PENNSYLVANIA

9171-A Roosevelt Blvd., Philadelphia, PA 19114	215-676-9494

SOUTH CAROLINA

243 King Street, Charleston, SC 29401	803-577-0175

TENNESSEE

4811 Poplar Ave., Memphis, TN 38117	901-761-2987

TEXAS

114 Main Plaza, San Antonio, TX 78205	210-224-8101

VIRGINIA

1025 King Street, Alexandria, VA 22314	703-549-3806

CANADA

3022 Dufferin Street, Toronto, Ontario, Canada M6B 3T5	416-781-9131

¡También somos su fuente para libros, videos y música en español!

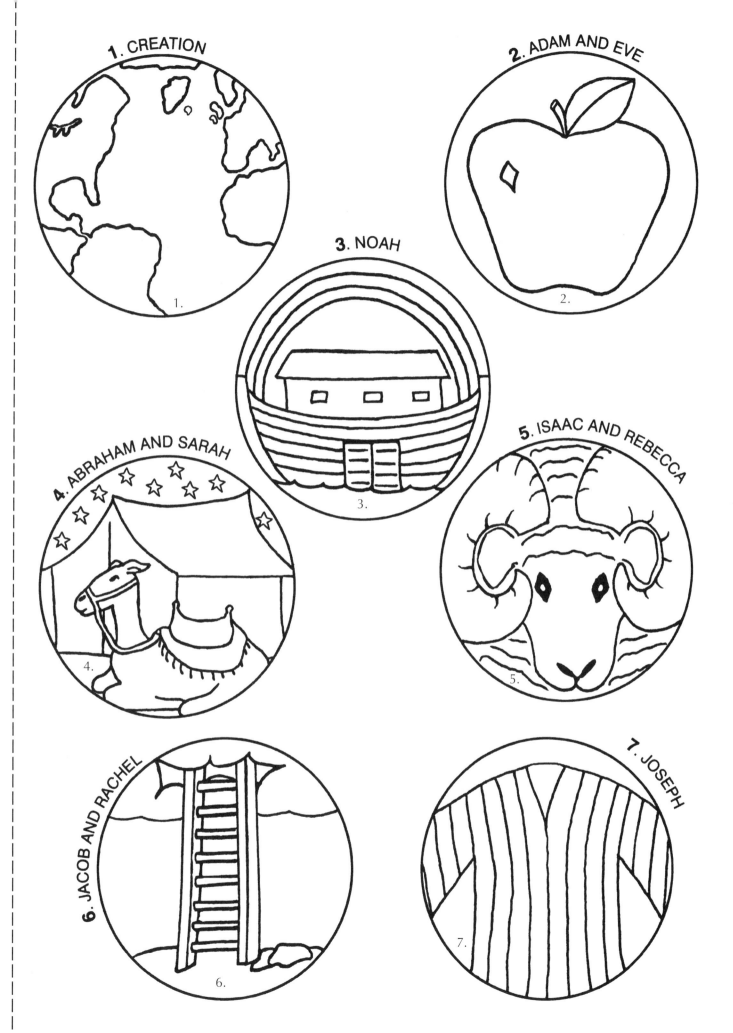

1. CREATION

1.

2. ADAM AND EVE

2.

3. NOAH

3.

4. ABRAHAM AND SARAH

4.

5. ISAAC AND REBECCA

5.

6. JACOB AND RACHEL

6.

7. JOSEPH

7.

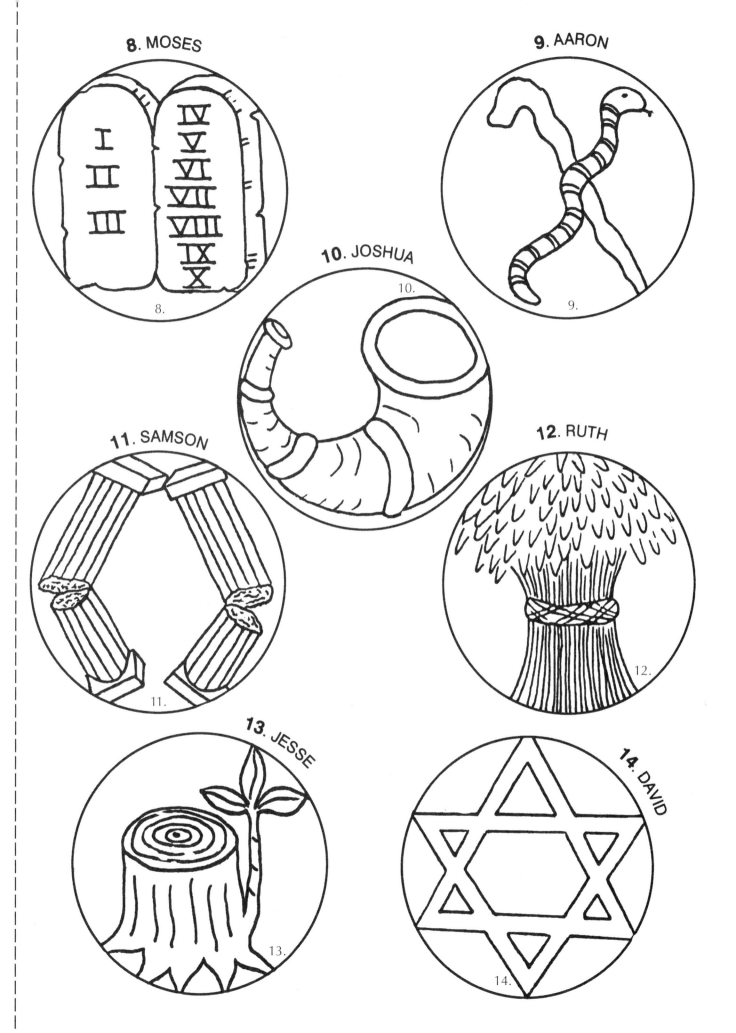

8. MOSES

9. AARON

10. JOSHUA

11. SAMSON

12. RUTH

13. JESSE

14. DAVID

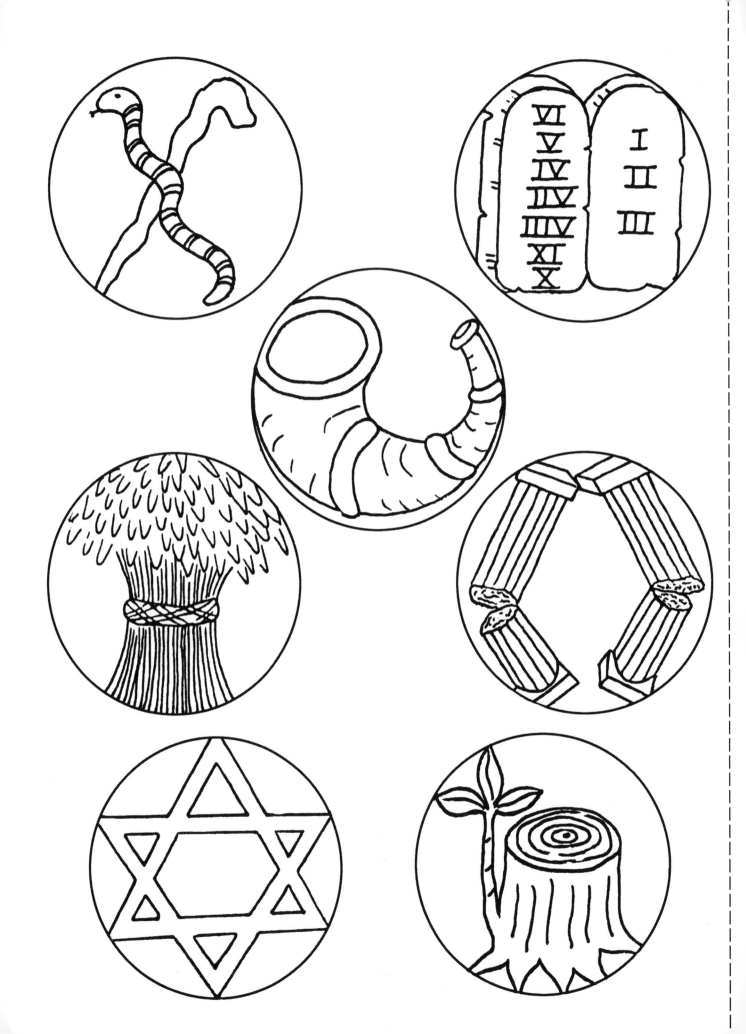

15. SOLOMON

15.

16. ELIJAH

16.

17. ISAIAH

17.

18. DANIEL

18.

19. JONAH

19.

20. ZECHARIAH AND ELIZABETH

20.

21. JOHN THE BAPTIST

21.

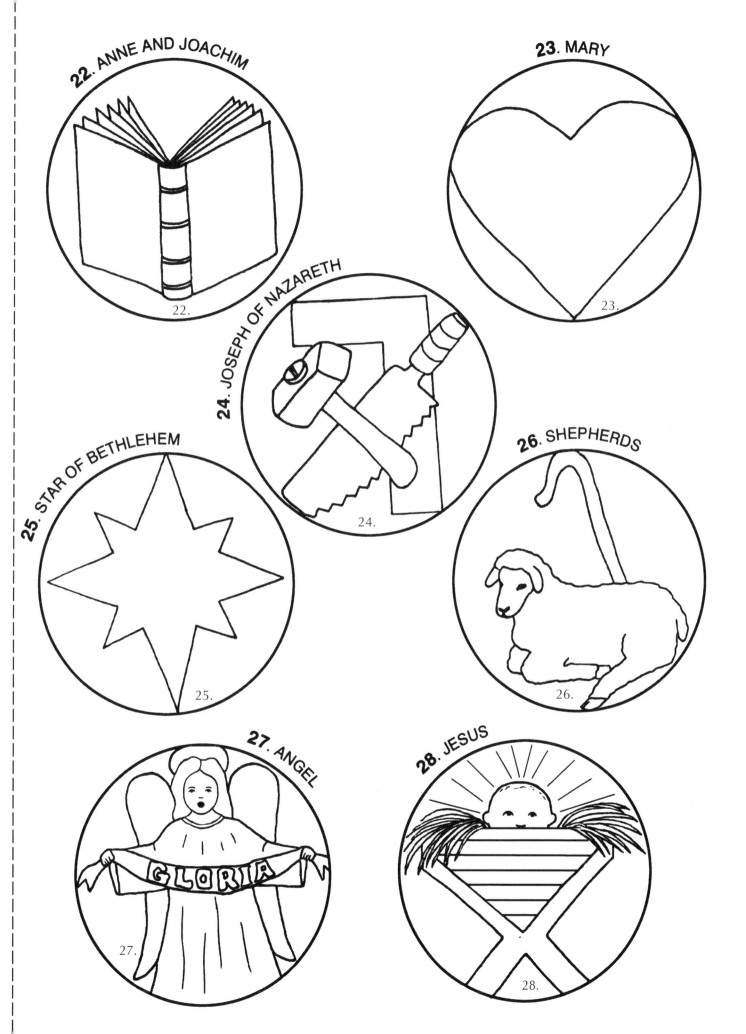

22. ANNE AND JOACHIM

22.

23. MARY

23.

24. JOSEPH OF NAZARETH

24.

25. STAR OF BETHLEHEM

25.

26. SHEPHERDS

26.

27. ANGEL

GLORIA

27.

28. JESUS

28.